YOUR KNOWLEDGE HAS VALUE

- We will publish your bachelor's and master's thesis, essays and papers

- Your own eBook and book - sold worldwide in all relevant shops

- Earn money with each sale

Upload your text at www.GRIN.com and publish for free

Jitendra Jain

How Europeanization is heading towards a clustered convergence?

GRIN Verlag

Bibliografische Information der Deutschen Nationalbibliothek:

Die Deutsche Bibliothek verzeichnet diese Publikation in der Deutschen National-
bibliografie; detaillierte bibliografische Daten sind im Internet über http://dnb.d-
nb.de/ abrufbar.

Dieses Werk sowie alle darin enthaltenen einzelnen Beiträge und Abbildungen
sind urheberrechtlich geschützt. Jede Verwertung, die nicht ausdrücklich vom
Urheberrechtsschutz zugelassen ist, bedarf der vorherigen Zustimmung des Verla-
ges. Das gilt insbesondere für Vervielfältigungen, Bearbeitungen, Übersetzungen,
Mikroverfilmungen, Auswertungen durch Datenbanken und für die Einspeicherung
und Verarbeitung in elektronische Systeme. Alle Rechte, auch die des auszugsweisen
Nachdrucks, der fotomechanischen Wiedergabe (einschließlich Mikrokopie) sowie
der Auswertung durch Datenbanken oder ähnliche Einrichtungen, vorbehalten.

Imprint:

Copyright © 2006 GRIN Verlag GmbH
Druck und Bindung: Books on Demand GmbH, Norderstedt Germany
ISBN: 978-3-656-40583-2

This book at GRIN:

http://www.grin.com/en/e-book/211768/how-europeanization-is-heading-towards-
a-clustered-convergence

GRIN - Your knowledge has value

Der GRIN Verlag publiziert seit 1998 wissenschaftliche Arbeiten von Studenten, Hochschullehrern und anderen Akademikern als eBook und gedrucktes Buch. Die Verlagswebsite www.grin.com ist die ideale Plattform zur Veröffentlichung von Hausarbeiten, Abschlussarbeiten, wissenschaftlichen Aufsätzen, Dissertationen und Fachbüchern.

Visit us on the internet:

http://www.grin.com/

http://www.facebook.com/grincom

http://www.twitter.com/grin_com

How Europeanization is heading towards a clustered convergence?

Index

Introduction

The term Europeanization is becoming more and more fashionable. Some scholars including Samuel Huntington argue that citizens of European states increasingly identify themselves as such, rather than French, German etc.[1] Various theories and terminologies are used to describe Europeanization and its future .But such attempts have failed because this term does not have single or precise meaning. Europeanization has reached a crucial stage. Scholars are debating about the trends and directions of Europeanization. Convergence, Divergence, Similarities or Differences are some of the flashpoints of discussions. Such discussions have raised various questions about Europeanization. e.g. What is the emerging picture of Europeanization and how this polarization is taking place?

This work aims to find out answers to these questions and more precisely about direction of this process i.e. how Europeanization is heading towards clustered convergence? I also narrate emerging faces and trends in Europeanization.

What is Europeanization? This work is aiming for description of present trend in Europeanization. I will begin with discussing some definitions about Europeanization. I also agree that Europeanization is not an easy term to define. Hence I will proceed further to discuss and debate about Europeanization in nutshell. How Europeanization takes place? After describing Europeanization I will proceed to discuss the logic adopted by various scholars to facilitate Europeanization.

Forthcoming section of the term paper deals with five faces of Europeanization as discussed by Johan Olsen.[2] Discussion about Europeanization would be incomplete unless a reference is made to globalization. Hence in this paper I also intend to describe relationship between Europeanization and globalization. Concluding chapter is about

---

[1]Huntington, Samuel P.: Kampf der Kulturen
Übersetzt von: Fliessbach, Holger
Siedler Taschenbücher, München, 1998
[2] Olsen, Johan P.: The Many Faces of Europeanization
Arena Working Papers, WP ½ , 2002

ground realities and attempts to find a viable description of future trend of Europeanization.

This work is primarily based on the essays of Tanja Boerzel et al[3] and Johan Olsen.[4]In addition to these two essays, I have taken help from several other resources and working papers.

1   Deriving meaning of Europeanization

1.1 Defining Europeanization

Europeanization doesn't have a single or precise meaning. It has been often used to describe various aspects and changes happening in Europe. Various scholars have made attempts to define Europeanization in various ways. Here I would like to narrate some of them. Ladrech defines Europeanization as „...an incremental process reorienting direction and shape of politics to the degree that EC political and economic dynamics become part of the organizational logic of national logic of national politics and policy making."[5] He suggests that Europeanization is a process and it is getting bigger and bigger. He also says this process is shaping logic of national politics and this process is influenced by actions of EC. Risse, Cowles and Caporaso define Europeanization as "the emergence and development at the European level of distinct structures of governance, that is, of political, legal and social institutions associated with the problem solving that formalize interaction among actors, and of policy networks specializing in the creation of authoritative European rules."[6] They describe Europeanization as creating structures of governance at European level in form of political, social and legal institutions, which leads to more interactions among participants and these institutions help them in solving common problems. These networks lead to

---

[3] Börzel, TA and Risse, T: When Europe Hits Home: Europeanization and Domestic Change
European Integration Online Papers Vol. 4 No 15
[4] Ibid.2
[5] Ladrech, R: Europeanization of Domestic Policies: The case of France
Journal of common Market Studies (1994) P. 70
[6] Risse, Cowles and Caporaso : Europeanization and Domestic Change
In: Transforming Europe. Europeanization and Domestic Change
Cornell University Press, Ithaca (2001) P.3

creation of European rules which are binding on all actors. Hix and Goetz define Europeanization as "a process of change in national institutional and policy practices that can be attributed to European Integration."[7] They understand Europeanization as a process of change happening due to European Integration. Börzel defines Europeanization as "a process by which domestic policy areas become increasingly subject to European policymaking."[8] She describes Europeanization as a process in which domestic policymaking is influenced by European policymaking.

The above mentioned definitions convey different connotations and sometimes contradictory aspects about Europeanization. These definitions also don't give an exact and a precise description of Europeanization. Analysis of various definitions helps us to derive a viable definition of Europeanization, such as "Europeanization is domestic change caused by European Integration and policy making at European level". However I admit that this definition is also not exhaustive enough to cover all aspects of Europeanization.

1.2 Conceptualizing Europeanization

As we saw earlier, there are numerous definitions of Europeanization. But these definitions are not exhaustive enough to cover all aspects of Europeanization. Hence the term Europeanization requires further elucidation and conceptualization.

Dyson and Goetz narrate the difficulties relating to precise understanding of Europeanization, when they describe how the term was used in a number of different ways, "......it is sometimes used narrowly to refer to implementation of EU legislation or more broadly to capture policy transfer and learning within the EU. It is sometimes used to identify the shift of national policy paradigms and instruments to the EU level (other).... times it is used in a narrower way to refer to its effects at the domestic level.... or in a more expansive way to include affects on discourse and identities as well as

---

[7] Hix and Goetz: Europeanized Politics. European Integration and National Political System
Frank Class, London(2001) P. 27
[8] Börzel: Toward convergence in Europe?
Institutional Adaptation to Europeanization in Germany and Spain
Journal of Common Market Studies (1999) P.574

structures and policies at the domestic level."[9] They say that Europeanization not only refer to implementation of EU directives but also include policy transfer and learning within EU. Europeanization is also related with shift happening in national policy in favour of policy at EU level.

Bullet and Gamble also explored wider conceptualization of Europeanization but ultimately considered it to be ".... a situation where distinct modes of European governance have transformed aspect of domestic politics."[10] Europeanization is considered as a situation in which European governance have transformed the character of domestic politics.

Fundamentally, they wished to explore existence of Europeanization at the member level but realized that outcomes are not inevitable and rely on interactions between member states and the domestic and EU levels.

Dyson explained, "...Europeanization remains relatively new theoretical interest and has produced more questions than answers."[11] He is of the opinion that theoretical discussions about Europeanization have raised more questions and dilemmas rather than solutions.

Sharing same opinion Featherstone and Kazamias proposed that Europeanization was a "...........dynamic process unfolding over time" and through complex interactive variables it provided contradictory, divergent and contingent effects.[12]

They ultimately argued that Europeanization included both the domestic and EU levels of policymaking and stressed on the interdependence between the two.

[9] Dyson, K. und Goetz, K. : Germany and Europe : Beyond Congruence
Presented at Germany and Europe : A Europeanized Germany
Conference British Academy, 2002 P.17
[10] Buller, J and Gamble, A.: Conceptualizing Europeanization. Public Policy and Administration
Special Issue, Understanding the Europeanization of Public Policy, Vol.17 No. 2 PP 4-24, 2002, P. 17
[11] Dyson, K.: Introduction : EMU as Integration, Europeanization and Convergence
In Dyson, K. (ed.) European State and Euro
Oxford University Press , 2002 P.3
[12] Featherstone, K. and Kazamias, G. (Eds.) : Europeanization and Southern Periphery
Frank Class, London , 2001

1.3 Understanding Europeanization

The provisional definitions described in previous chapters raise various questions about nature of Europeanization and to be more specific, what kind of change is Europeanization and what not.

Europeanization could be interpreted in many ways. Europeanization is not static but a dynamic term. Recently a lot of research has been done about the term Europeanization. Scholars of European Integration increasingly deploy the concept of Europeanization to assess the European sources of domestic policies. Recent research on Europeanization focuses on wider changes in organizational logic of national politics and policymaking.

Radaelli rightly says that in order to avoid the danger of conceptual stretching, one need to specify not only what Europeanization is but also what it is not. Europeanization should not be confused with convergence, divergence, harmonization or political integration.[13]

Convergence might be a consequence of European Integration, but it must not be used synonymously with Europeanization because there is a difference between a process and its consequence. Harmonization of national policies is very often the basic aim of European Integration but empirical studies suggest that Europeanization often manifests another and different impact of European requirement on domestic policies.

Europeanization is somehow related to outcome of the European Integration process. Relationship between Europeanization and European Integration is further elaborated in forthcoming chapters.

1.4 Debating Europeanization

Here once again I refer to viable definition of Europeanization stated in earlier chapter i.e. "Europeanization is domestic change caused by European Integration and policy making at European level". Europeanization is reflected in the domestic change. Degree of Europeanization is measured by the level of domestic change. Hence I proceed to discuss, how domestic change happens.

Two conditions must be fulfilled, when we expect domestic change. They are:

---

[13] Radaelli, Claudio M.: Whither Europeanization? Concept stretching and substantive change

a. Europeanization must be *inconvenient.*[14] European level policy must be incompatible with policy at domestic level. Unless there is presence of some element of incompatibility, change can not be expected. There must be certain degree of *"misfit"* between the process at European level and the process at domestic level. Nature and level of *'fit'* or *'misfit'* factor determines adaptation pressures.

b. Existence of misfit factor alone is not sufficient and *per se* it does not lead to Europeanization. Hence second condition is about presence of facilitating or mediating factors, which respond to adaptation pressures. These factors are actors as well as institutions. Facilitating or mediating factors help to achieve Europeanization.

Adaptation Pressures

There are two theories, which provide explanations about adaptation pressures.

Rationalist institutionalist perspective follows *"logic of Consequentalism"*. This logic explains that misfit between European and domestic processes create both opportunities and constraints. And hence domestic impact depend on capacity of actors to exploit these opportunities and avoid constraints. They emphasis on existence of institutions and regard them as main facilitators of domestic change.

Other sociological institutionalist perspective follow *"logic of appropriateness"*: They argue that socialization and collective learning process result in norm internalization and development of new identities. Here strong presence of cooperative political as the main mediating factor is recommended.

These two logics are not mutually exclusive. Attempts to deal with them exclusively or their exclusive deployment should be avoided, because very often they occur simultaneously and describe different faces in a single process of adaptation change.

European Integration online Papers, Vol. 4, 2000, P. 5,6
[14]Börzel, TA and Risse, T: When Europe Hits Home: Europeanization and Domestic Change
European Integration Online Papers Vol. 4 No 15,2000, P.1

1.5 Comparing Europeanization and Economic Integration

Europeanization and European Integration are not one and the same.. There are similarities as well as differences. For example Europeanization or European Integration could be labelled as a process or as a consequence, depending on circumstances.

Definition given by Hix and Goetz, stated in earlier chapter, describe European Integration as an independent variable and changes in domestic systems or Europeanization as dependent variable. Here Europeanization could be understood as the process of downloading European Union directives, regulations and institutional structures to domestic level. However this is valid if Europeanization is always an outcome of the changes at domestic level. But on occasions, when domestic level affects European Integration, then the variables are reversed. Here Europeanization could be interpreted as uploading to the EU common beliefs, informal and formal rules, discourse, identities and vertical and horizontal policy transfer. The distinction between European Integration and Europeanization as dependent and independent variables is not valid.

1.6 Identifying Europeanization with Globalization

The term Globalization should be understood before we make an attempt to understand Europeanization. Economic pressures from Globalization are closely connected with increasing Europeanization.

Europeanization should not be misunderstood as regional variation of Globalization. In fact Europeanization could be described as protective layer against the negative impacts of Globalization for member countries. Europeanization has tremendously helped member countries' competitiveness through discipline of monetary integration and economies of scale contributed by Single European Market. European Economic policies have helped member countries by adopting various measures such as common agricultural policies, anti-dumping measures and common industrial policies.

Various member countries have felt the economic constraints arising from globalization differently depending upon their economic vulnerabilities.

Greater the degree of economic vulnerabilities, more are the economic constraints. These economic constraints have forced some countries to go for

Europeanization, because they were in search of protective layer against negative impact of globalization.

2 Assessing performance of Europeanization

2.1 *Measuring* the *i*mpact of Europeanization on Domestic Policies

Börzel and Risse describe three degrees of change in national policies of member states that might take place due to Europeanization.[15] They are as follows:

Absorption: Member states are able to incorporate European policies or ideas and readjust their institutions without substantially modifying their existing structure. The degree of domestic change is low.

Accommodation: Member state are able to accommodate Europeanization pressure by adapting existing processes without changing their essential features and without damaging collective understanding. The degree of domestic change is modest.

Transformation: Member states replace existing policies by new ones to the extent that their essential features and the collective underlying understanding fundamentally changes. The degree of domestic change is high.

2.2 *Emerging* Faces of Europeanization[16]

a. Geographical Boundary of Europe
Recently it has been observed that very often the term "Europe" has been used with reference to the European Union and its members. As described in

---

[15]Börzel, TA and Risse, T: When Europe Hits Home: Europeanization and Domestic Change
European Integration Online Papers Vol. 4 No 15,2000,P.10
[16]Olsen, Johan P.: The Many Faces of Europeanization

beginning more and more citizens of Union are introducing themselves as inhabitant of Europe.

But one can argue that European transformations are not limited to the European Union. Impact of these transformations is immense. They influence not only member countries but non-member countries as well e.g. cross border relations. Hence proper understanding of ongoing changes is must for non-member states, transnational institutions, regimes and organizations.

Johan Olsen argues that European Union agreed for enlargement without precise calculations of consequences.[17] Enlargement of European Union requires a large amount of resources. In addition to huge cost, it requires certain important changes to be done by prospective member states. This leads to new opportunities and challenges for member states.

EU documents portray enlargement as based upon liberal democratic principles. EU Enlargement is consistent with Community values and interest of existing as well as applicant countries. Here it is important to know possible tensions, which may arise due to norm-driven behaviour. Participants are often aware of consequences of such norm-driven behaviour.[18]

It is also suggested that enlargement may be decided through application of basic norms, but the distribution of the cost of enlargement may be decided through self-interested calculations and bargaining.[19]

b. Creation of a system of governance at European level

Europeanization is also described as the Institutionalization at the European level of a unique system of governance with common institutions and authority to make, implement and enforce Europe wide binding policies.

Europeanization includes both the strengthening of an organizational capacity for collective action and the development of common ideas, like norms and collective understanding regarding citizenship and membership.[20]

Arena Working Papers, WP ½ 2002, P.4

[17]Ibid.,P.7

[18]Ibid.,P.8

[19] Olsen, Johan P.: The Many Faces of Europeanization
Arena Working Papers, WP ½,2002, P.8

[20] Checkel, J.T.: The Europeanization of citizenship?
In Cowles M. G. , Caporaso J. A. and Risse T. (Eds.),Transforming Europe;
Europeanization and Domestic change

Here the challenge is to design an institutional framework, which is agreeable to all participants. European Union is assumed to be involved in a continuous search for "the right formula for building lasting and stable institutions" in order to improve the functionality, legitimacy and creditability of the institution of governance.[21]

In order to create a stable platform, participants (member countries) must prepare a common minimum program. Then they have to develop an institutional framework to realize it.

Rokkan[22] (1999) suggest four dimensions of institution building:

Regulatory institutions: Building a unified administrative and military apparatus for protection of the population, territory and external borders, including ability to generate resources for such common purpose. e.g. NATO, Europaguard etc.

Socializing institutions: developing, through education and socialization, a territorial identity and a cultural community with a sense of belonging, emotional attachment and a shared code of meaning. e.g. Erasmus Program

Democratic institutions: creating democratic citizenship, representative institutions, equal right of political participation, legitimized opposition, organized political parties and for a public debate and popular enlightenment. e.g. European Parliament, European Commission

Welfare institutions: developing social and economic citizenship and rights and a community that accepts the collective responsibility for securing more equal life chances for citizens through the means of public service, reallocation of resources, and the regulation of the use of private resources. e.g. EZB, EFTA, OECD etc.

c. Domestic impact of single point governance

Here Europeanization deals with those domestic changes, which happens due to development of a system of governance at European level. Domestic

---

Cornell University Press, Ithaca, NY, 2001a P.180
[21] Patten, C.: Sovereignty, democracy and constitutions-finding the right formula
Schuman Lecture, Australian National University, Canberra , 2001
[22] Rokkan, S.: State Formation, Nation Building and Mass Politic in Europe
Oxford University Press, Oxford, 1999

changes are regarded as dependent variable. Domestic impact of decisions at European level depends on pattern of adaptation. And Europeanization as adaptive process is guided by various concepts.

Two basic concepts for understanding Europeanization as adaptive process are:

experientia learning and competitive selection

experientia learning: Institutional change on the basis of experiences with, and interpretation of, how relevant actors in the environment react to alternative form of domestic change. Here the actions are assessed and successful ones are repeated.

Competitive selection: environmental imperatives drive the change. Efficient institutions survive, others disappear. Actors are selected or elected in the beginning and their growth or survival depends upon their performance and how well they fit in changing circumstances.

Variation in degree of adaptation and uneven responses should be expected in political setting like European Union. This is primarily because European institutions are unevenly developed. As a result adaptation pressure may vary. Another reason for such variation is European political order itself. European political order is product of long and varied history. Some actors are proud of their achievements. They want to protect their system and do not allow penetration to take place. Some are eager to go beyond the past. Penetration in domestic system is happening in some areas easily, at the same time there is strong resistance in some areas.

There are some convergences in policy-making areas. However, by and large there is no revolutionary change in any of the national system and no major convergence toward creating a common institutional model. Structural divergence is present. However there is substantial increase in contact and competition among national models.

Europeanization as domestic impact is not limited to structural and policy changes. European values and policy paradigms are close to some (varying) degree internalized at the domestic level, shaping discourses and identities.[23]

---

[23] Checkel, J. T.: The Europeanization of citizenship?
In Cowles M.G., Caporaso J.A. and Risse T. (Eds.), Transforming Europe:
Europeanization and Domestic Change.

Likewise common concepts of appropriate fiscal behaviour, taxing and "sound" money and finance have developed at the elite level.[24]

d. Exporting European institutional systems

Historically Europeanization has been described as spread of lifestyle, i. e. spread of forms of life and production, food & drinking habits, religion, language, political principles, institutions and identities typical of Europe to the rest of the world beyond European territory.

This spread of European system can be better understood as *diffusion* process. This term is borrowed from epidemology. Proper Understanding of spread of a system requires in-depth analysis of various aspects, such as pattern of diffusion, durability of its impact, factors contributing to its spread etc... Here in this paper I am not discussing them in detail, because my discussion is restricted to description of the Europeanization trend.

Earlier spread of European models of organization and governance has taken place in form of colonization, coercion and imposition. European institutional system had penetrated and changed the traditions and institutions in other continents. They undermined the importance of established systems and such spread resulted in confrontations.

Diffusion has also taken place in form of imitation and voluntary borrowing from a successful civilization. They copied European arrangements because they understood their functionality, utility or legitimacy.

e. Political unification of Europe

It describes Europeanization as a political development making Europe a distinct, coherent and strong political identity. Member states are submerged into a single political space and a system of governance. For all meaningful purposes this entity acts as a whole.

Cornell University Press, Ithaca, NY, 2001a
[24] Radaelli, C.M.: How does Europeanization produce domestic policy change
Corporate Tax policy in Italy and the United Kingdom
Comparative Political Studies,1997

Internal boundaries are removed. External boundaries and controls are made stronger. Fragmented European states are unified and the boundaries of political space are extended beyond the member states.

One must understand that strong political Europe doesn't imply just maximizing territory, centre building, adaptation of national and sub national system of governance and export of European solutions. It also means the institutionalization of political borders, authority, power and responsibility. European Union enlargement will lead to increase in territory, population as well as resources. This unification will create more heterogeneity and hence will pose a challenge on unified governance. Unified governance mechanism will allow them to act in a more coherent way and play more significant role in global developments. Sometimes strong adaptation pressure may generate protest and resistance from member states and those others disagreeing with common policies. Strong adaptation pressures on domestic systems without adequate respect for local autonomy, diversity and protection of minority may provoke conflict and obstruction.

Export of European solutions to the world may prove success. But a stable and successful European development might depend on imports from other parts of the world.

3 *Concluding* Observations about the trend of Europeanization

3.1 Evaluation of Europeanization

It can be observed that Member states are following the path of EU polity. Europeanization on national polities is also visible. But changes at the EU level are much faster than changes occurring at the national level. Entire impact of constitutional amendments and revisions leading to institutional and procedural adaptation is not substantial. The strategies adopted by all national players do not reflect any major structural reorientation.

Some member states e.g. Germany and France have adopted proactive approach to Europeanization. Both countries are founding members of European Monetary Union. France had to undergo a transformation in its

14

monetary policy. Responses from many other member states have been lukewarm. Members have not yet incorporated any concrete adaptation strategy. However one could still observe shift in major policies of member states made under influence of European Union.

Active participation of European Union has resulted in evolution of culture and policies.

3.2 Convergence versus Divergence

The debate about convergence or divergence is confusing. It is not at all easy to describe the trend or the direction of Europeanization. Something that might look like convergence at macro level might have several feature of divergence at micro level.

European Monetary Union has led to policy convergence among member states with respect to inflation, deficit and independence of central Banks.

But member states do not have similar arrangements in economic and fiscal areas.

European Union rules demand convergence in policy outcomes e.g. low inflation and budget deficit. At the same time member state have discretionary powers with regard to certain measures they adopt to ensure proper compliance.

There are sufficient empirical studies to prove that the outcome of domestic effect of Europeanization have been somehow diverse. Convergence does not essentially leads to homogenization of domestic structures. Domestic change does not essentially mean complete rejection of national policies.

3.3 Convergence not moving towards one dominating Structure

Constitutional, institutional and administrative systems have not converged into one model for all member states.[25] One must admit that even though each of them was facing same kind of challenges, the degree of convergence among them is relatively small. Traditional national systems were flexible

---

[25] Mittag, Jürgen and Wessels, Wolfgang: The „one" and the „Fifteen"? The member states between procedural adaptation and structural revolution
In: Fifteen into one? The European Union and its member states
(Hg.) Wolfgang Wessels, Andreas Maurer & Jürgen Mittag
Manchester University Press, New York, 2003, P.444

enough and hence could easily face the new challenges. Incorporation of new competitive set up and procedure were rare.

Prima facie competitive pressures have lead to harmonization of matters in political spheres. Each member state is working hard in its own way to incorporate guidelines issued from Brussels. Some traditional key players have converted challenges into opportunities to strengthen their position in intra-state matters.[26] However this is not without ambiguities. It is too early to evaluate outcomes.

Modestly it could be argued that efforts of these participants have increased the complexity of national procedures but without damaging national system and also in harmony with Brussels directions. Hence this way along term trend towards new institutional *equilibria* both at the national and at the European level is established.[27]

Autonomy of central banks as a consequence of EMU, the changing role of parliament in their relationship with government with an urge to reduce democracy deficits etc.[28] – such small measures might be regarded as tiny steps of very little importance to the established patterns of the national systems, which has simply been adopted. Member states were able to incorporate European policies without modifying their structure. The degree of domestic change could be termed as "Absorption".[29]

3.4 Dynamics of Adaptation Process

However this adaptation process and its dynamics in the long term could converge into one specific type of Member State for the union. The aftermath from EU developments might be of more importance than what we imagine now. Variations in the Member States' might become thinner. This process might not lead to development of a uniform type of Member State, but naturally historical differences would lose their importance and thereafter EU polity would affect national structures and habits.

---

[26] Ibid. , P.444
[27] Ibid. , P.444
[28] Ibid. , P. 445
[29]Börzel, TA and Risse, T: When Europe Hits Home: Europeanization and Domestic Change European Integration Online Papers Vol. 4 No 15,2000,P.10

The impact of such process on long-term relevance of Member States should also be examined. Broad involvement of many participants and search for consensus could give birth to a political and institutional culture different from an adversarial culture. Consensual democracy will be of importance not only at EU level but also at national level. The Community as a system might reinforce a dominant culture i.e. European Culture.

Perhaps such a convergence might make life of EU system easier and beneficial to all participants.

3.5 Fazit: Europeanization *heading towards clustered Convergence*

A "misfit" between European level and domestic process is essential for expecting any change. Adaptation pressures alone are not solution. There must be some mediating factors at domestic level. These mediating factors may be actors as well as institutions. For example transformation in Germany in financial services sector took place in response to growing competitive pressures from European capital market integration and was not initiated by European Commission but by domestic actors.[30]

Theoretically there are two logics, which enable domestic change. Rationalist institutionalism follows logic of resource distribution emphasizing absence of veto points and existence of institutions as main facilitators of domestic change. Sociological institutionalism emphasizes on socialization and learning. They strongly recommend presence of cooperative political as the main mediating factors.

These logics and pathways are not mutually exclusive. They often occur simultaneously and characterize different phases of process of adaptation change. Sometimes they may relate to each other in sequential way. Logic of consequentalism exogenizes preferences and identities, where as the logic of appropriateness endogenizes them.

Recent trend in Europeanization indicate that it might lead to convergence in policy outcomes, but at the best to "Clustered Convergence" and at the same time divergence in policy processes. There are several empirical examples to

---

[30]Schmidt, Vivian A.: Europeanization and the Mechanics of Economic Policy Adjustments
Boston University, Boston, 2001, P.11

justify this. For example in telecommunication sector one can see convergence happening as three important EU member countries namely Germany, France and Britain have liberated this sector almost entirely under influence of EU policies. But one can observe divergence as distinctiveness remains in the policy making institutions with Britain giving more freedom to regulatory agencies in term of licensing and retail pricing than either France or Germany.[31] There is reasonable degree of convergence in financial services sector in these three countries, as they all have liberalised in the same way. But here is also substantial divergence in policy making areas. British regulatory is based on public law; the French is based on SEC structure and German on federal agency.[32]

---

[31]Schmidt, Vivian A.: Europeanization and the Mechanics of Economic Policy Adjustments
Boston University, Boston, 2001, P.11
[32] Ibid.,P.11

Bibliography

Börzel, T. A.: Toward convergence in Europe?
Institutional Adaptation to Europeanization in Germany and Spain
Journal of Common Market Studies, 1999

Börzel, TA and Risse, T: When Europe Hits Home: Europeanization and Domestic Change
European Integration Online Papers Vol. 4 No 15

Buller, J and Gamble, A: Conceptualizing Europeanization. Public policy and Administration Special Issue, Understanding the Europeanization of public policy, Vol. 17 No 2 PP 4-24, 2002

Dyson, K. and Goetz, K.: Germany and Europe: Beyond Congruence
Presented at Germany and Europe: A Europeanized Germany
Conference British Academy, 2002

Dyson, K: Introduction: EMU as Integration, Europeanization and convergence, In Dyson, K. (ed.) European States and Euro
Oxford University Press, 2002

Featherstone, K. and Kazamias, G. (Eds.): Europeanization and the Southern Periphery, Frank Class, London, 2001

Fuhrmann, Nora: The Impact of Europeanization on Endangering Politics and Policy in Europe, University of Toronto, 2004
Goetz, K. H. and S. Hix: Europeanized Politics. European Integration and National Political Systems. Frank Class, London, 2001

Huntington, Samuel P.: Kampf der Kulturen
Übersetzt von: Fliessbach, Holger
Siedler Taschenbuecher, Muenchen, 1998

Howell, Kerry: Developing Conceptualizations of Europeanization and European Integration, Mixing Methodologies, Sheffield, 2002

Karabelias, Gerassimos: European Integration and South-Eastern Europe Observations and Suggestions, Ottawa, 2003

Ladrech, R.: Europeanization of Domestic Politics and Institutions: The case of France.
Journal of Common Market Studies Vol. 32 No 1 pp69-87 1994

Mittag, Jürgen and Wessels, Wolfgang: The „one" and the „Fifteen"? The member states between procedural adaptation and structural revolution
In: Fifteen into one? The European Union and its member states
(Hg.) Wolfgang Wessels, Andreas Maurer & Jürgen Mittag
Manchester University Press, New York, 2003

Olsen, Johan P.: The Many Faces of Europeanization
Arena Working Papers, WP ½, 2002

Radaelli, Claudio M.: Whither Europeanization? Concept Stretching and substantive change
European Integration online Papers, Vol. 4, 2000

Risse, T, M. G. Cowles and J. Caporaso: Europeanization and domestic change, in: Transforming Europe. Europeanization and Domestic Change
Cornell University Press, Ithaca, NY, 2001

Rokkan, S.: State Formation, Nation Building and Mass Politic in Europe
Oxford University Press, Oxford, 1999

Scharpf, Fritz W.: European Governance: Common Concerns vs. The Challenge of Diversity, Cologne, 2001

Schmidt, Vivian A.: Europeanization and the Mechanics of Economic Policy Adjustments
Boston University, Boston, 2001

Thielemann, Eiko R.: The Price of Europeanization: Why European Regional Policy Initiatives are a Mixed Blessing

Vink, Maarten: What is Europeanization? and other Questions on a New Research Agenda
University of Bocconi, Milan, 22-23 November 2002